Zoom in a Kart

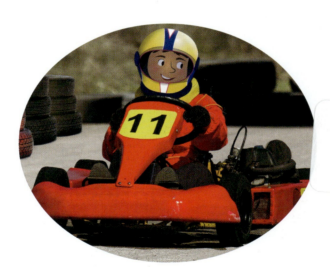

Written by Charlotte Raby

Illustrated by Ángeles Peinador

Collins

part of the kart

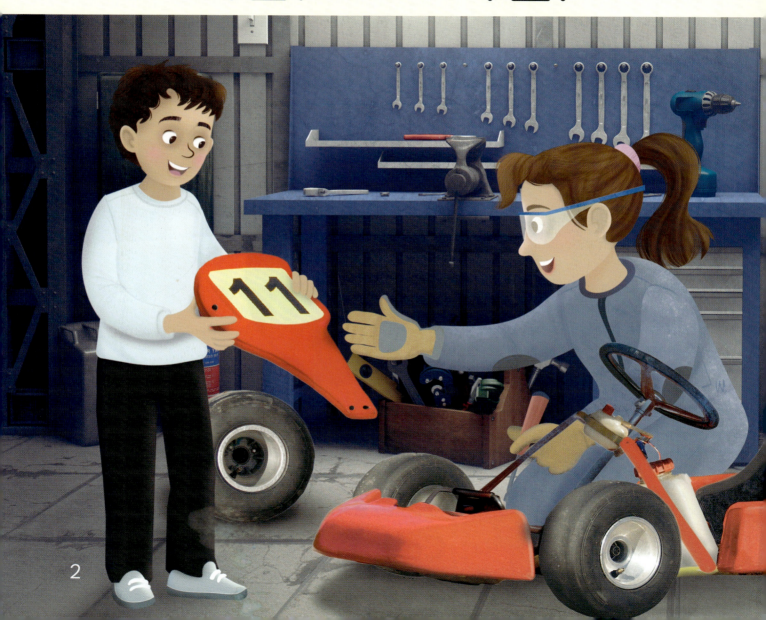

coat and boots

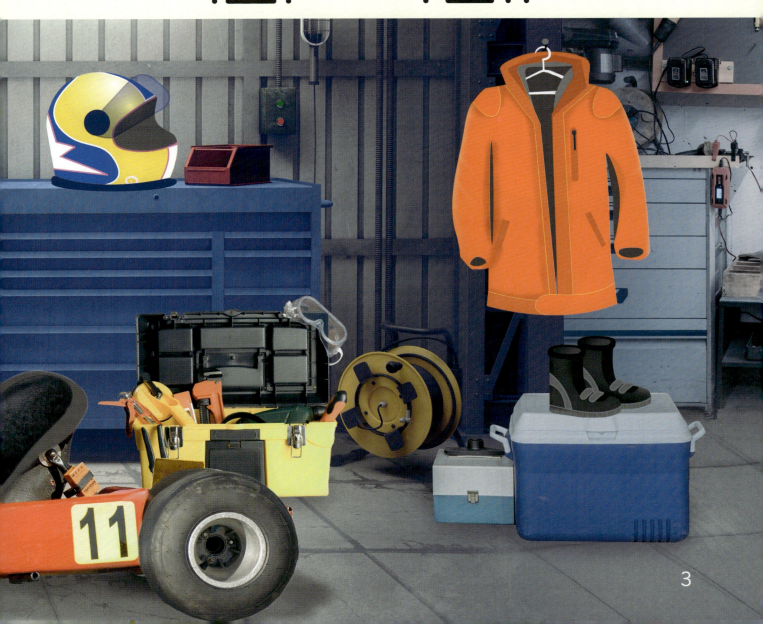

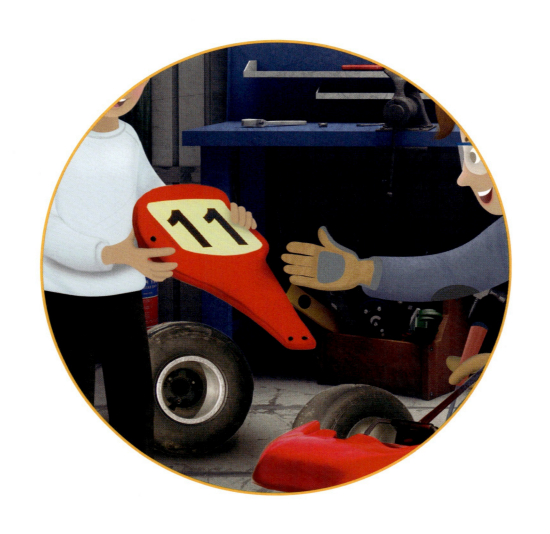

part of the kart

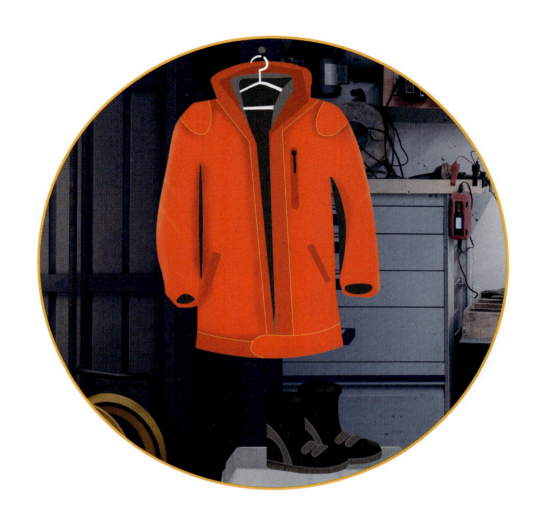

coat and boots

a red kart

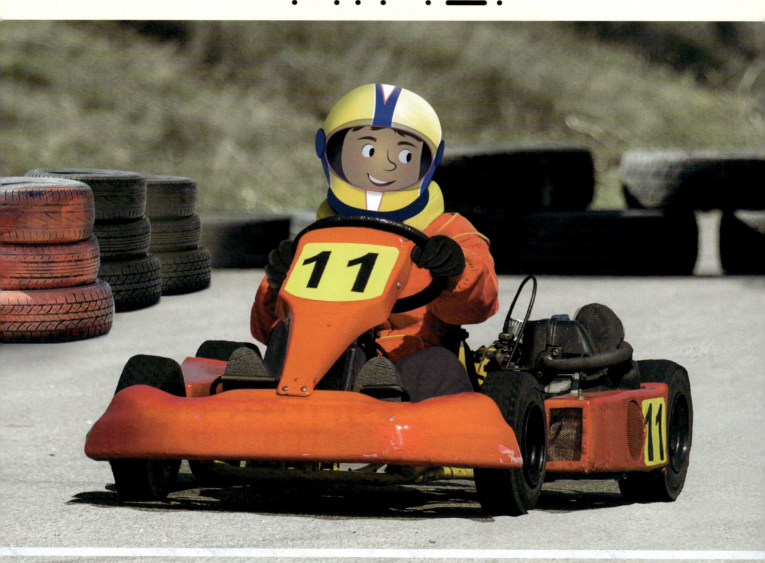

toot and beep

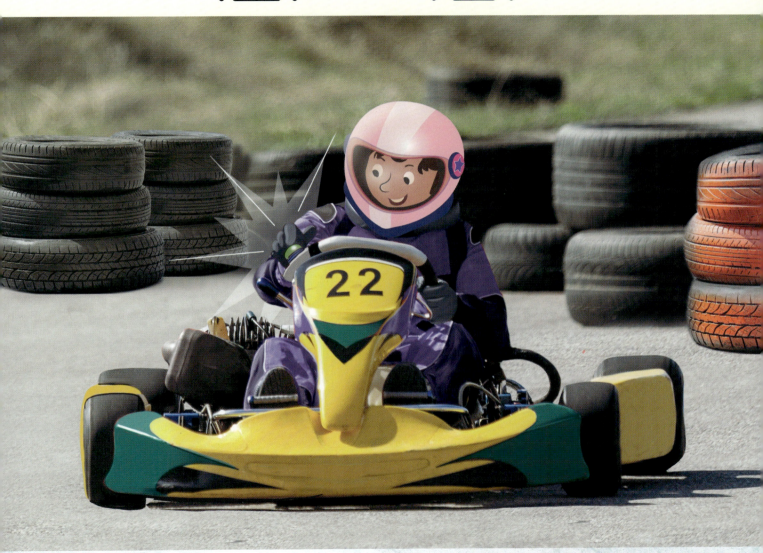

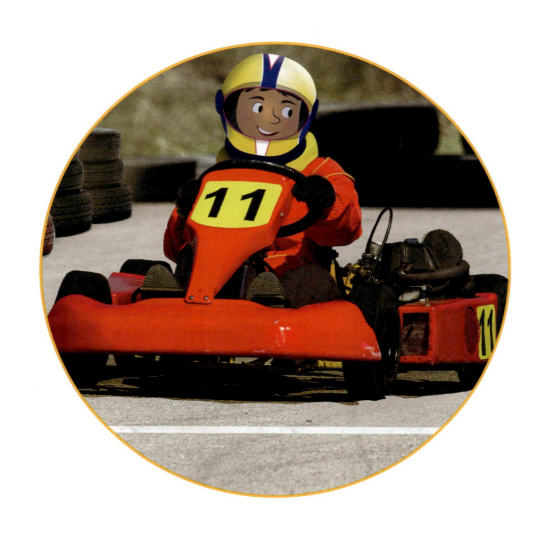

a red kart

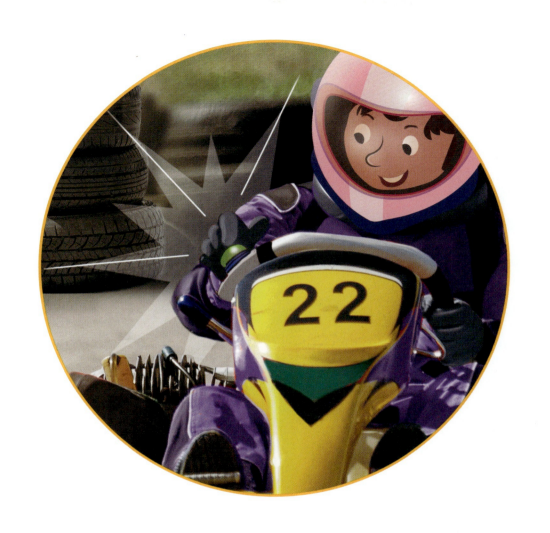

toot and beep

zoom to win

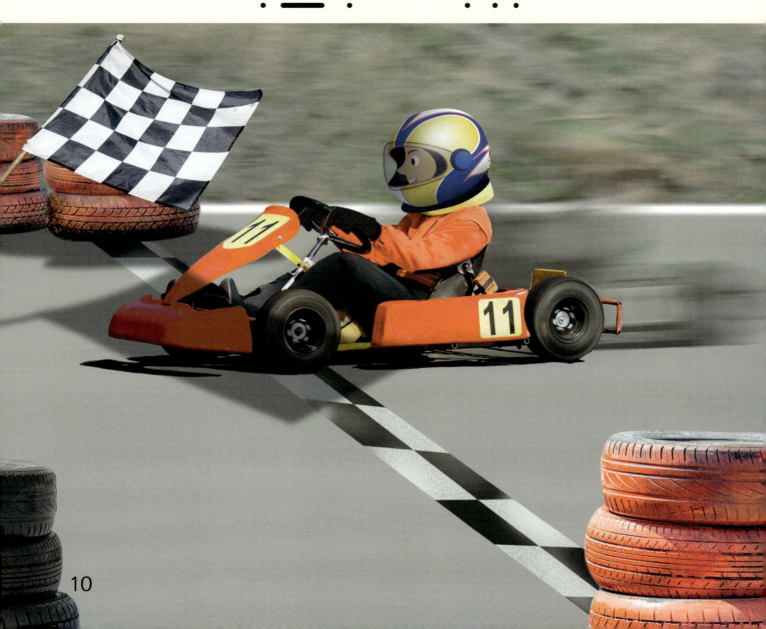

arms up

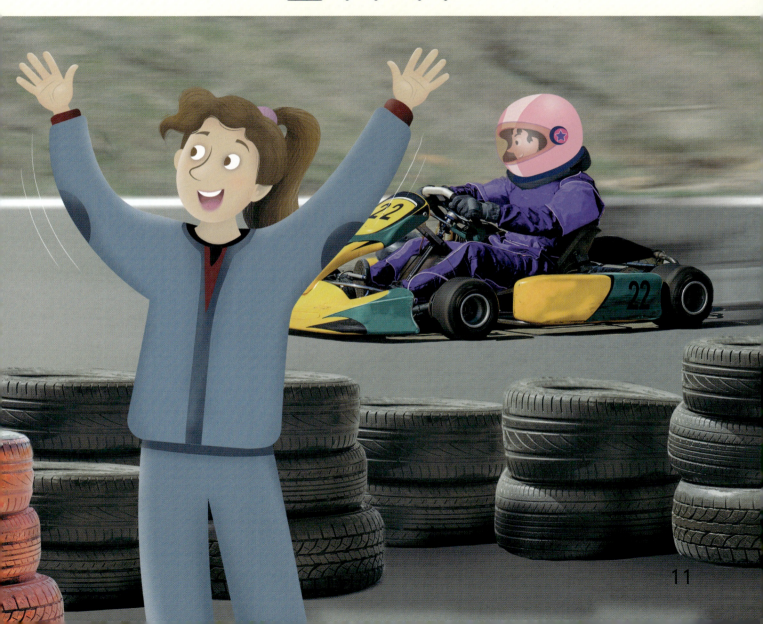

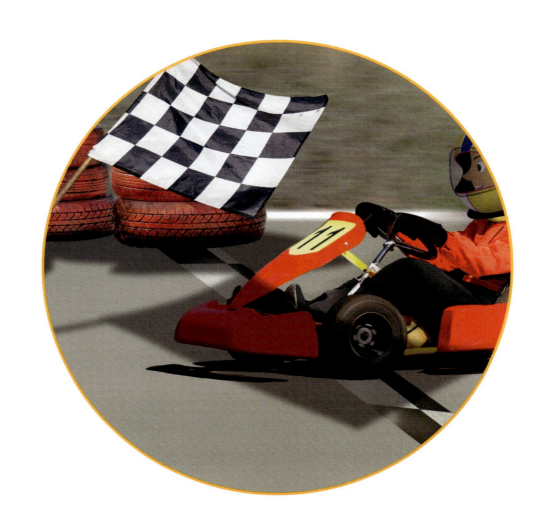

zoom to win

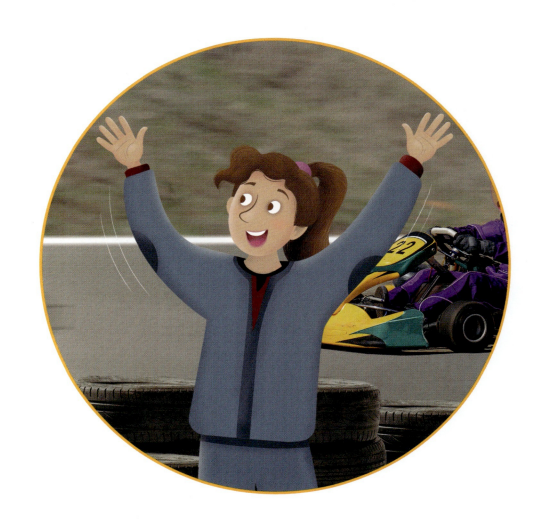

arms up

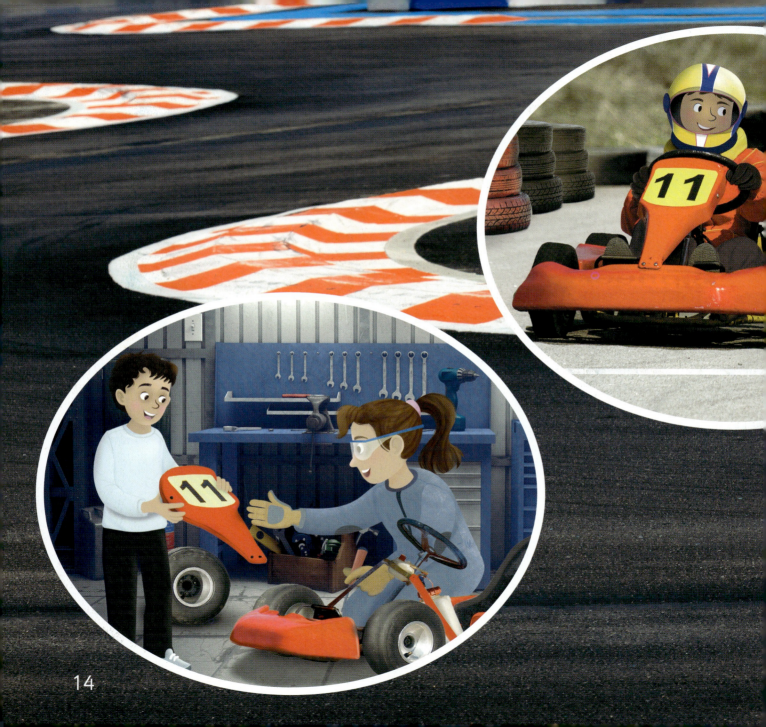